Hell Is Not Always Hot

Sometimes the air conditioning is on!

Taedra J Morris

Cover design by Taedra Morris

Interior design by Taedra Morris

Edited by Meyonne Spencer

Illustrations by Fotolia

Photographs by Atlanta Mediaworks

Hell Is Not Always Hot
Copyright © 2009 by Taedra Morris
Published by Taedra Morris
All rights reserved.
ISBN - 13: 978-0-615-33757-9
ISBN – 10: 0615337570
Library of Congress Control Number: 2009943699

Printed in the United States of America

"One woman's triumph over her struggle and finding her glory in a relationship with God"

I would love to hear your thoughts.

Share your comments with me at:
www.hellisnotalwayshot.com

Acknowledgements

Heaven is right here on earth!!! This book is dedicated to you! It was given to me by the awesome God that I serve. God the Father, God the Son, and God the Holy Spirit. Without You, where would I be? Thank you Father for always loving me, even when I didn't love myself. God works with us in our lives, in His order and in His time. I know that I am no greater than what I believe! Well, I now believe that I am great!

We have to be emptied in order for God to fill us up. God will fill our mind with what He wants us to think. He will fill our heart to make us complete. God knows what we need in order for us to walk in His light. I challenge you today to let Him fill you up! But, please believe that you will have to go through something in order to be emptied from your worldly desires and strongholds. I thank my family for always encouraging me, even when I didn't want to receive it. I love you Dad, I love you Mom, I love you Brother, to my Sister, I love you, and Daijah my "Bushes," I love you! You guys are the reason my heart beats! My Sisters in Christ Brandy, Charity, Cody, and Kim where would I be without you all! I love you dearly. Tiffany you are my sister and an inspiration, I love you! Letta, your life is a testimony that must be shared. It's time to be set free! I will always love you. Sharrie, keep sharing your story; others will be set free because of what you went through. I love you! To all my family and friends, I love you and thank you for standing by my side when I needed you most. To my vocational rehabilitation crew thanks for your acceptance and for your friendship. To my dear friend Elvis, you already know! It's your turn! I love you! Pastor France A. Davis, I love you so much and please know that you are an inspiration to me. To my church family at Calvary Baptist Church in Salt Lake City, Utah, thank you for your love. Bishop Eddie L. Long, thank you for your vision and your obedience. Your walk and your words kept me in the right direction. Minister John Gray, thank you for your commitment to the singles ministry, God used you in such a way that changed my life! Minister Lori Allen, my life has truly been blessed from your ministry, thank you! To my church family at New Birth Missionary Baptist Church in Lithonia, Georgia, thank you all for passing the peace, encouragement, and kind words, I love you all! It's finally over! I now have JOY!

Grandma

Dear

Grandpa

Their descendants will be known among the nations and their offspring among the peoples. All who see them will acknowledge that they are a people the Lord has blessed." Isaiah 61:9

Preface

Hot as hell

Picture Hell. It was heavy and strong! It poured down like rain in the middle of a rainforest! All I could see was darkness and quick flashes of light before my eyes. Every time I opened my eyes they would burn. My vision became blurred and I tried to keep my eyes closed as much as possible, but I needed to see where I was going. I was running trying to get away, but I had nowhere to go. I ran until I could run no more. I couldn't get a break from the feeling that my flesh was burning. Heat was coming from every direction. Everywhere my foot landed I grew hotter and hotter. The darkness kept getting darker. There was nowhere to hide and I was all alone! The feeling of something wet covered my body, but there was no water in sight. My body ached in excruciating pain. I had no more strength to run. Where was I running to? I fell to the ground but there was no ground to catch me. I just kept falling! It was too dark to even see my hand in front of my face. The flashes of light were overshadowed by the fire that kept burning me. I reached out for something, someone, or anything that I could grab onto, but there was nothing! Every time I extended my arm, the burning sensation would increase; but I had to bear the pain to stop my fall. I wrapped my arms around my body and felt the raw open flesh. I touched my shoulder and could feel the muscle; my skin was melting. There were holes in my body where the fire that poured down like rain burned through my skin. The pain was agonizing. Suddenly, I crashed into what I thought was the ground. My body was one with the concrete and I slowly lifted my head. The fiery rain poured down . . . I was surrounded by darkness. The heat radiated from every direction. Even underneath me! The temperature of this place was hot! More than 240 degrees! I tried to get up, but my body was so weak I quickly fell back to the ground. I was covered in blood and I had no more energy. I couldn't live like this anymore! So I laid there hoping that I would burn up and die. But it never happened, you see reader, I was already dead. I was in Hell!

What you just read was an example of what hell could look like. What does this really mean? What makes hell, hell? Is it the temperature and extreme heat that makes hell, or is it the situation that you are in? Have you ever said to yourself I don't want to go to hell? Imagine a world with no trees. Think about it, this would mean no shade anywhere and not a shadow in sight. Have you ever missed your shadow? A world without shadows could be hell. Imagine a world with nothing to stand taller, bigger, or stronger than you to block the heat and sunlight from beaming down on you . . . even for just a moment. What would you do if I told you that you might have already been there, or that you might be there right now. You would probably think that I am crazy, but keep reading and you will see that hell might just be in your living room or your bedroom where you lay your head every night. What is the reading on your thermostat? I'll bet that it's not more than 240 degrees, but yet your mind and your thoughts could be so dark that you don't even realize that you're in hell. Hell with air conditioning!

I came up with the title, "Hell Is Not Always Hot, Sometimes the air conditioning is on" because I lived in hell, constantly worried about my hair. I settled for less in life, not knowing that I deserved all that God has for me. I was in hell, crying in my living room, bedroom, or car. But I was never hot. I always had air conditioning. I'm sharing my story in hope that I can help others get through their struggles. I know that if I can reach just one person and restore their confidence, God will say job well done!

It all started about twelve years ago. I was about twenty and started losing my hair, that's when the struggle started. I became depressed but hid it well. I wore wigs and weaves to hide what was going on, but deep inside I was dying and crying every night. At twenty-four, I was diagnosed with Poly Cystic Ovarian Syndrome (PCOS). In some ways I was relieved to know that there was something wrong with me. However, on the other hand I didn't know quite how to deal with knowing that I had a "syndrome." Every day was a struggle, but I have finally accepted my hair loss and I recently shaved off all of what was left of my hair. Glory be to God! He gave me peace about it all! I don't worry anymore what people think or say about me. I now know that I am beautiful with or without hair. I'm sharing my story in hopes of becoming a motivational speaker for people who may be going though something that is holding them back from being who God has created them to be. God gave me this book to write and I am so thankful that you have decided to take this journey with me....

CONTENTS

Chapter 1

What Has To

Happen

God has been calling me to follow Him for a very long time. I hid from Him, just like I hid the fact that I was losing my hair from my friends and family. I was so glad to find out that a thing called weave and ponytails were invented. Believe me, I was the first in line! In fact, some of my friends would call me Sally toupee! LOL They never knew why I always had a hair piece on. Don't get me wrong, it was all in love because they were known as chin strap, wide nose, and chiclets! I had to go there Tiff! I grew up with Tiff and through her love of God she has been an inspiration to me. Her bright smile (and two front teeth shaped like chiclets), light up whatever room she enters. "Chin Strap," had a chin that just didn't stop growing as child and we were concerned that his chin weighed his head down so much that he wasn't able to keep his head up. So we named him chin strap! LOL, (this is an inside joke and in no way intended towards anyone who actually wears a chin strap). "Wide nose," has just that a wide nose. We let him lead the way when we go anywhere, because he had a good "sense" of direction! LOL I am cracking myself up! Anyway, I was known in my church for always looking my best from my hair to the clothes I wore. I relied on the hair dresser to do her best to disguise the fact that my hair was thinning. I had more hair on my head than a shaggy dog. I believed that if my hair wasn't laid at all times I wouldn't even be worthy of a conversation with another person. Losing my hair held me captive for way too long. The enemy influenced me to believe that it was powerful and that I was not worthy of all that God has promised me. I was persuaded to believe that being a woman without hair meant that I wasn't a complete woman.

I remember getting my hair styled in a ponytail and it was pulled so tight that I couldn't even think. The tension on my hair made my hair follicles go into shock. My hair was never really that strong so it didn't take much. I remember when I took the ponytail out. I was left with a small circular bald spot at the crown of my head. I didn't take it that seriously because I always thought it would grow back. It came to a point that I could not cover up the bald spot unless I wore ponytails, so I had to continue wearing them. My hair loss soon became a spiral affect. The hair follicles were not strong enough to hold the new growth, and as a result the falling hairs continued across my head. After I was diagnosed with PCOS, I started doing research and came across the symptoms. Hair growth and hair loss was listed as some of the symptoms. Hair loss was not common with PCOS, but there were a few that it affected. I fell into that few. I hid the fact that my hair was falling out until I could no longer hide it with ponytails. The pain that I felt was unbearable. Women, we know that men love hair, so of course, I felt like I would never find a husband who would love me without hair. There were countless nights where my pillowcase was drenched from my silent tears. I could cry at the drop of a hat. My hair loss was always on my mind. There were many days that I would drive to work and could barely see through my tears. When I got to work I would have to sit in the parking lot and get myself together, before going inside. I would sit there and look at myself in the mirror, and I wouldn't step out of my car until my face displayed happiness. I would put on that smile, but I was really dying inside. Everyday my heart ached with pain, especially when I would look in the mirror. I hated what I looked like with paper thin hair. The way beautiful women were portrayed in our society during these years were always with long hair. My definition of a beautiful woman was not what I saw in the mirror. There were times when I would rather stay in the house where I was comfortable rather than go out and face the world. Eventually, I stopped going to the beauty salon because I was too embarrassed to let other women and people in the shop see my head. I let my friends do my hair and learned how to do it on my own. I just started trying different styles and actually got pretty good at it. I would tell my mother that if I ever got a husband, he would never see my head. I was determined to hide this fraction of my life from everyone. I remember the day when I couldn't hide it anymore by just adding hair. I put a perm in my hair in order to straighten it in the same fashion that I always did. By this time I guess my hair had lost all strength. I jumped in the shower to wash the perm out of my head, which was my regular routine when I permed my hair.

Imagine this…

I was washing my hair with my eyes closed. When I opened my eyes I saw black stuff all over the bottom of the tub. I was startled because I didn't know what was in the shower with me. I put my hands in my hair to see if the shampoo was rinsed out and when I pulled my hands down in front of my face my hands were full of my hair. I was in shock! So I rubbed my hair again just to see if I was losing my mind or really losing my hair. Once again, my hands were full of my black hair that I was trying so hard to hold on to. I jumped out of the shower and looked in the mirror. My hair had fallen out in patches. I started screaming and began to cry. I couldn't think about anything but what people would think if they saw me like this. I needed my hair! I sat down on my bed and couldn't do anything but wonder why I had to lose my hair. Between the tears and the screams from being in shock my mother came running upstairs to find out what was going on. She saw me and instantly said, "What happened?"

She has always been the "snap out of it" one. She wanted me to stop crying so she could assess the situation. I knew she was nervous but it never showed in her reaction. She encouraged me saying, "Taedra, your hair will grow back. Why don't you just get it cut real short?" At the time I was too overwhelmed and shocked at what just happened to me. I didn't want to receive her encouragement at all. I needed to know why this happened to me. I was in no way wanting to figure out solutions. I felt like my life was coming to an end. I couldn't see all of the blessings that God still supplied me with. All I could focus on was why did God take my hair away. Sometimes we can be so ungrateful and trapped by the negative aspects of our situations. If we actually take time to think about what we do have, we will live a happier life. I didn't think about the fact that I was still living, breathing, healthy, I had a roof over my head, and I had friends and family that still loved me regardless if I had hair or not. I had high hopes that it would grow back but it never did completely. My hair only grew back in patches and at times, I felt like life was just not worth living.

In order for you to do what God tells you and live in the likeness of our Father, something has to happen. You have to be broken, crushed, let down, disappointed, abused, and left all alone. God knows our breaking point and He uses it to His advantage. He gets us right to the edge until we have nothing or no one to turn to, but Him. He knows what we go through. You have to learn to praise Him through your time of crisis. You are only in a crisis because God is near, He wants the ultimate praise and He wants you to know who it is that will lift you up when no one else can. He is the one that allowed your husband to leave with that other woman.

You depended on him too much anyway. So, your focus was not on God. You thought you could not live without the love of your wife or your girlfriend. They didn't leave you because they were fed up with you, they left because God has a plan for your life and they may have been in the way. Or perhaps God separated you temporarily until He's finished with both of you. Maybe it's your mother, you thought that a mothers' love is all you ever needed to feel whole, but you could never get her to show you an ounce of love. It's not your mothers' fault. Forgive her! You have to surrender to God in order to know the plan that God has for your life and the real reason why your mother was never there for you. She may not have been capable of loving you the way God wanted you to be loved at the time. He knew you'd turn to Him. God wants you to desire His love like we desire the love of human flesh. No man or woman can love you enough. God is love and enough if we submit to His love; He will send people to us that will love us with His unconditional love.

And so we know and rely on the love God has for us. God is love. Whoever lives in love lives in God, and God in him. 1John 4:16

Chapter 2

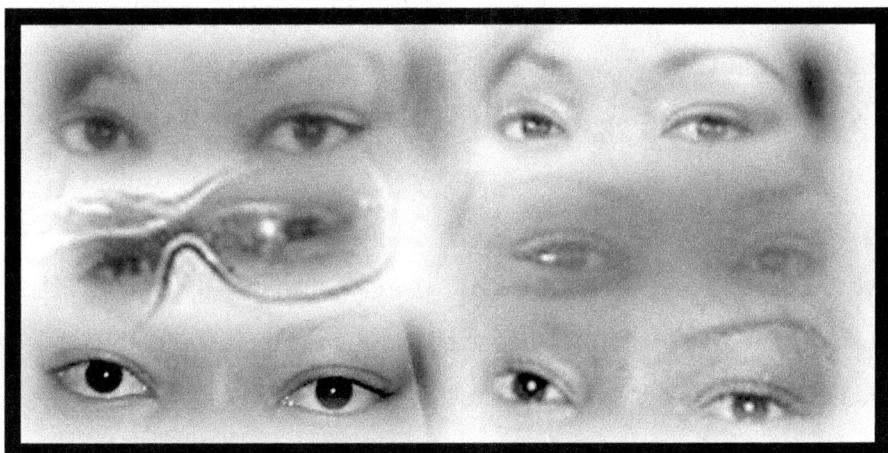

Facade

I was so ashamed and did not want anyone to see how I really looked without hair. I had made up my mind that I was going to live with my parents forever. I knew that they loved me unconditionally and believed that they were all I had. I went into a deep, silent depression. I felt as though I didn't want to live any longer because life just wasn't worth living. I had many thoughts of suicide and actually tried to figure out how to take my life without anyone knowing that I had actually killed myself. I would purposely not wear my seatbelt when I was driving, because I knew that I would rather die if I were ever in a car accident. I prayed that I would develop cancer or some other disease that caused hair loss. That way, I believed that if I had cancer, I could tell people that the cancer was the reason my hair fell out. I was extremely depressed and I found it difficult to focus on anything long enough to get my mind off of my hair. During this state of depression, I never wanted to be in a situation where I had to explain that I lost my hair, so I made sure that I never got too close to anyone, especially a man! I even hid my hair loss from my family for a long time. It reached a point where I had to start wearing wigs. I felt like I had hit rock bottom when I had to buy a wig. I couldn't even walk into a wig store without feeling that people were looking at me and laughing at the fact that I had to wear a wig. My mother and father tried desperately to encourage me. I remember being in California and visiting a wig store that was as big as a warehouse. It was so overwhelming and all I saw was hair everywhere I looked. Now that I think about it, I should have been rejoicing for all that hair, but my pity wouldn't let me. I was mad and ashamed that I even had to be in there. Exposing my bald head, for the first time, to the store personnel was one of the hardest things that I have ever had to do. While I couldn't stand wearing wigs, I bore the pain. It was better than not having any hair on my head at all. I tried really hard to hide the fact that I was wearing a wig. I would put them in ponytails, swoop the bangs to the side; I tried anything that made my wigs look more natural. It satisfied me for the meantime. However, I really wasn't hiding anything! I remember a time when I fixed my hair just right and felt as though no one would be able to tell that I had fake hair on. I was on my way out of town and was standing in the airport. The waiting area was crowded and there were no empty seats anywhere for me to sit... where I would not be subjected to anyone looking at my hair. I was forced to stand and ended up standing in front of a young man that was sitting down facing me. I stood there and waited for my name to be called so that I could get on the flight. While I was standing there, I looked down and noticed that the man was looking directly at my hair. I became disturbed and quickly looked away, trying to act like it didn't bother me. I took another look in his direction and once again he was staring like he had never seen hair in his life. I became frustrated and started asking myself, what is he looking at? My mind started going wild and my frustration turned into anger. This man would not stop looking at my hair even for a second. I felt my face tighten and started to frown at him, giving him a look with wide eyes that said why are you looking at me? To my surprise the harsh expression on my face didn't affect him at all. He continued to stare at my hair and didn't care that my blood was boiling. I thought to myself, should I snap at him and ask him if he's ever seen a fake ponytail, or should I just tell him to stop staring at me? My lips grew tighter and my fist slowly formed into a ball. I was ready to hurt this man if he didn't take his eyes off my hair in the next two seconds. Right when I was about to go off and make a spectacle of myself, the Holy Spirit gently told me to turn around. At the time I didn't know that the voice I heard was the Holy Spirit, but now I do. I turned around and looked up. I was standing directly underneath a TV screen. The man was not staring at my hair after all! He was watching the TV that I was standing underneath! I couldn't believe it, I had made up in my mind that this man was consumed with my hair. In reality I just had a fight with the artificial intelligence (AI) in my own head. (See chapter 3) I took a deep breath and said to myself, Taedra you need to calm down. I was about to create a scene in the airport that day, that would have more than likely turned ugly, because I was so angry. I was convinced that my hair was the center of attention. When in reality it was only the center of my attention. I had grown so paranoid about my appearance and I didn't even realize it.

My advice to you... get to know God so that when He speaks to you, you will recognize His voice. Secondly, stop being consumed with things you cannot change. Live your life without worry, because God will always get you through.

Therefore do not worry about tomorrow, for tomorrow will worry about itself. Each day has enough trouble of its own.

Matthew 6:34

I decided to try hair restoration products that I had seen advertised or read about. This was a joke! I tried more than 15 different products. All I got…were allergic reactions. No hair at all! Not a strand! I did, however, muster up enough courage to go to a hair restoration doctor. I went to the appointment alone and when the "so called" doctor examined my head, he told me that there was nothing he could do for me. He explained that the procedure he uses takes hair from the back of your head and transplants it to the front. He said that my hair in the back would soon fall out and that there would be no purpose of putting it in the front because it would fall out there, too. I couldn't believe that he said this to me. I was absolutely devastated, because the commercial said that they could make hair grow back, and that was all I wanted to hear. I jumped up from the table, gathered my things and ran out of the office. My eyes swelled with tears and I told myself I would never do that again. Once again, I fell into a down spiral of depression. I put my hopes in man and had great expectations that a doctor could restore my hair and my life. Oh, how soooo wrong I was!

We must stop putting our faith in man and calling on our friends and family to get us through life's challenges. The only man we need to put our faith in is God, His son, and the person that will sustain us, the Holy Spirit. The Holy trinity is your remedy! Without a shadow of a doubt, it is the complete package that is guaranteed to see you through any situation in which you find yourself stuck. I'm so thankful that the facade I hid behind came to an end. I can now be who God called me to be. No more hiding thoughts of despair and fearing that someone might just find out who the real me is. I encourage you right now to put down the facade. Be who God called you to be. His hand is upon you and He will lead you every step of the way.

The hand of the LORD was upon me, and he brought me out by the Spirit of the LORD... Ezekiel 37:1

Don't be afraid to trust that God will see you through any situation. God is not like the facade that you continue to hold on to. He is everlasting and His glory endures forever. He chose you for such a time as this right now. He wants to use you, but you must surrender it all to Him.

Chapter 3

Strongholds

I s there a barrier that needs to be broken in your life? I had one. God gave me my "get out of hell free card" and He has one for you, too.

My story happened like this...

On December 11, 2008, God delivered me from the stronghold that shaped my life for the past twelve years! I can now say that I am living in Heaven on earth! Can you say that? Understand that it's your choice! You can believe in the AI or you can believe in the Alpha and Omega (AO). Minister John Gray, singles ministry leader at New Birth Baptist Church in Lithonia, Georgia, explained it in a simple way that I could understand. I want to share it with you!

So here we go....

AI stands for *artificial intelligence*. AI is who you listen to when you are not in God's divine order and not in His will. AI tells you to be afraid of your circumstances. It also wants you to doubt yourself. Don't get me wrong! Sometimes the AI will also make you think and feel successful. It will give you a good boost every now and then. If the AI sounds good to you, it's just not your time, God is still working out some issues with you and that's ok. You have to remember what goes up in the AI must come down, because the AI is never definite. It doesn't want you to live in heaven. Do you wonder why your relationships never work out? It's because you are listening and living with an AI influence. The AI will always stand in the way of every relationship, goal, focus, and other things that God has destined for your life. Know this... the AI does not discriminate because of your race, creed, status or religion.

You may be homeless and someone gave you this book or you may be very successful and decided to buy it for yourself. However you received a copy of this book, please be sure to read it and encourage someone you know to get a copy for themselves. I believe that you have just stepped into your miracle if you really take time and receive the words written on these pages. Please know that you have to go through some difficult times in order for God to trust you with His fruits of the Spirit that He has waiting for you.

Now on the other hand, AO means the Alpha and the Omega! Alpha described in the dictionary is the first letter of the Greek alphabet. It is something that is first; it is the beginning. Omega is the twenty-fourth and last letter of the Greek alphabet. It is the extreme or final part; the end. God is the Alpha and the Omega. He is the beginning and the end!

He said to me: "It is done. I am the Alpha and the
Omega, the beginning and the end. To him who is thirsty I
will give to drink without cost from the spring of the
water of life. Revelations 21:6

Where were you before you were born? Where do you go when you die? If you don't know this now, get to know God, your relationship with Him will show you the truth. Try thinking with an AO influence, it will lead you into the direction in which the AI told you to be afraid. The AO will encourage you when you feel like you have nothing. If you surrender to the AO you will never go back to AI.

Do not conform any longer to the pattern of this
world, but be transformed by the renewing of your mind.
Then you will be able to test and approve what God's will is-
his good, pleasing and perfect will. Romans 12:2

AO is your comforter, your healer, and your sustainer. God said that He wants the ultimate glory, the glory at the beginning and the glory at the end. The battle is in our mind; thinking with the AO in the forefront will lead you to your destiny. Trust in God and let Him lead each step you take. Stop worrying about what you can't change. Don't ever give up because it will all be worth it! Your future is God's past! You still have a future! He has a plan for your life! No matter how long you choose to prolong what God has ordained for your life, He will always make sure that he gets His way. God wants to use you in this time of your life. Let go of your thoughts, fears, discomforts and strongholds. Always remember that God is your number one source and that He will supply all that you need.

> *But seek first his kingdom and his righteousness, and*
> *all these things will be given to you as well.*
> *Matthew 6:33*

If you feel like you can't go on any longer, you feel empty, at your wits end or you just can't take it anymore, please stop right now and ask God to fill you up. *"Father*

God, right now I ask you to fill the emptiness. Erase the pain and give me the peace that only you can give. Give me what I need to keep pushing toward your light. I don't see you, but I know you're there. I feel your presence and I need you now more than ever. I'm afraid to let go and to walk in your likeness, but I know that you are with me. I know that with you, I can overcome anything. Nothing is too hard for you Father and I thank you for your glory. I thank you for your strength, I thank you for your patience and I thank you for your mercy. Thank you Father; you are truly the reason why I live. In your precious and most holy name I pray this prayer. Amen."

It doesn't matter what you are going through, just make sure you go through it! Embrace it. Remember that it will all be worth it in the end. Whatever you have lost, God will restore. You cannot be delivered from anything if you're not going through something. I thank God for my deliverance. God did what no man could do for me. I doubted myself every day. My parents who I adore and love more than I love myself could not get me to realize that I was beautiful with and without hair. The very two individuals that brought me in this world could not convince me that I was more than hair. My ex-boyfriends couldn't love me enough to make me feel whole. My friends couldn't persuade me to walk out the door of my house without any hair. I've searched the world and found that there is nobody like my God. He deserves all the glory, the honor, and the praise for my deliverance. I am so grateful for knowing who He is and knowing that He is real.

Here's what happened...

The day before I was set free of the strongholds that held me captive, I attended a singles ministry meeting at New Birth. If you ever have a chance to visit this church, I encourage you to make it a priority. God's presence was so vivid that night that it is literally unexplainable. God used Minister Gray to show me how to knock down the walls in my life that have been holding me captive for more than twelve years. I am grateful to Minister Gray for being an obedient vessel. I believe that this was my moment. It was my time to know that the battle of my life was over. My life has finally begun. After thirty-one years of living, I can now say that I live with purpose. Until recently, my daily battle was just walking out my front door and facing the world. My self-esteem was very low; however, I don't believe that anyone could really see how I felt about myself. I concealed my self-doubt and shame so well that no one that I met was aware of the silent war raging inside. It was as though I was putting a blanket over an erupting volcano, hoping that I could hide the potential expulsion of hot lava. The battle was all in my head just as yours may be. I now know that I was in a fight with myself.

March around the city once with all the armed men.
Do this for six days... Joshua 6:3-20

This was the Fall of Jericho. That night we were led to do like the people of Jericho, we walked around the sanctuary, which symbolized the wall that was holding us back from receiving God's promise. We walked, walked some more and praised God for all of His glory. God was so present that it felt like He was walking right next to me. A sweet spirit filled the atmosphere. It was an unstoppable spirit that you would want to take with you everywhere you go. I believe that this was the same spirit that the people of Jericho probably felt when they were walking around the wall. God spoke to each of us there who had an ear to listen.

What took place on that night was healing from longsuffering, restored confidence, revelation, changed lives and most of all God's children were led back to Him. I know that God is going to use everyone that received His grace that day in that sanctuary.

The very next day God led me to go to my job without wearing a wig. I couldn't believe that I had the strength to open my front door and the ability to expose the world to my real image. That which I had been ashamed of and hid for so many years, God instantly delivered me from it! I was actually doing it! I took a deep breath and stepped out the door. My first words of encouragement came from my dear friend and roommate, Charity. She looked at me with a smile and said, "You look good girl!" From that moment I knew there was no turning back. I said thank you and stepped out on faith.

If you have lost your hair or know someone that has, start or continue to encourage them. Even if they don't receive it now, please know that eventually they will. If you are going through anything that has defeated you and shifted the way you live, start encouraging yourself. Sometimes you can't wait for others because it might not happen. I have been walking with my head up from that day forward. I no longer feel that my hair defines who I am or what I deserve. I know that I am great and deserve what God has for me. You deserve the same. You no longer have to settle because you think you are only worth what is at the bottom of the stack. God has prepared a place for you at the top! It's not going to just drop on your lap, you just might have to fight for it. I believe that you have to first find God before you will be completely set free. Read Matthew 6:33 again. This is your first step to overcoming what is holding you back and to claim your "get out of hell free card." If Jesus had to go through hell, why do we think we deserve not to?

In fact, everyone who wants to live a godly life in
Christ Jesus will be persecuted. 2 Timothy 3:12

I want you to stop right now and thank God for the process that you went through, it may be the one that you are going through right now. Remember to keep your mind focused on Him and not your process. He will hold your hand and guide you step by step. You just have to let Him.

"This is what the Lord says to his anointed, to Cyrus, whose right hand I take hold of to subdue nations before him and to strip kings of their armor, to open doors before him so that gates will not be shut. Isaiah 45:1

There is nothing like sweet victory in the name of Jesus! I am walking in faith for the first time in my life. As humans, we make the mistake of making our problems and circumstances bigger than God. We have to stop doing this right now. Don't you know that nothing is too hard for God? You say it, but do you really believe it? What is holding you back from being who God has designed you to be? Think about it. You have a spiritual gift. Do you know what it is? If you don't know your gift then how are you going to live it out? You must change the way you think and the way you live. Your walk should look like Jesus, because He is our example.

Chapter 4

Lamp Shade
Over Your Light

When I was a child I remember being just as plump as I could be. Yes, I was a little butter ball! My brother would always tease me about being fat. I couldn't stand it then, but I laugh about it now. Being overweight as a child was hard to deal with. I knew and expected my brother to make fun of me, but I didn't ever want anyone else to do it. What I did as a child was turn my size into humor. I started making jokes about myself. I figured if I started the jokes and laughed at myself, others would not be laughing at me but laughing with me. I was good too! I really just repeated to my friends what my brother said about me, they all thought I came up with the jokes myself and that was exactly what I wanted. This made me feel better because I was the one to open up the "can of worms." I tricked everyone into thinking that my size did not matter to me. There wasn't any need for anyone to make fun of me because I already did it. I covered who I really was at a young age. I covered it so well that I won "school spirit" in junior high. I was big and popular on the outside, but really sad and small on the inside. Growing up, I went to a private school that was about twenty miles from my house. All of my friends lived near the school. I didn't really have many friends in my neighborhood. I became a home body and started staying in the house as I got older. I had friends at church but we all went to different schools. After my freshman year in high school I yearned to have friends that lived close to me. I begged my parents over and over to let me go to the public school that the neighborhood kids attended. The whole summer all I heard was "No!" Finally, my parents got sick of hearing my mouth and they gave in. I was on my way to West High, where I started to gain my identity. By this time I had slimmed down and thought I was the hottest thing walking! Life is really like a roller coaster. I went from one extreme to the other. High school was so much fun! I didn't have any worries. I had hair, I looked great, I was involved with my church, and I had friends that I loved. My light began to shine at this stage in my life. It was a dull shine but at least it started!

After high school, the roller coaster ride started to get a little scary. Inch by inch I was climbing up the ride of life. I felt myself getting closer and closer to college and the excitement and anticipation was so vivid. I was at the top of the roller coaster for the very first time and the excitement of finally making it up there was quickly overtaken by the unexpected drop that comes right after the peak of the ride.

Once again, I was in a new environment and had to figure out what lamp shade to put on to complement college life. I never got to the core of my problem. So every time my life changed, so would my lamp shade. I had to grow to a point where I wasn't covering up who I was. Lamp shades can change every day, but what matters is what's under the lamp shade. What's under your lamp shade?

Every time I step out of my door, I have to remind myself to let my light shine. Everyday I hated walking out the door, but I knew that I had to. I tried to let my light shine, but I never felt like I could completely be myself. I had several lamp shades over my light. If you think about the purpose of a lamp it's very simple. God wants us to be like lamps, but he wants to be able to pick out your lamp shade.

Think about this...

Lamps are used to light up a room, right? The shades that we put over the light, dulls the light and serves as a decorative purpose. It usually matches the décor in the room or makes some kind of statement, but in order for most people to notice that lamp, the light has to be on. In order for the light to turn on, the lamp has to be plugged into a source of energy. If you never plug your lamp into the outlet that has the power it will never turn on. You can flip the on switch but you will never get light. Well, our light is similar to a lamp.

We get dressed and make ourselves presentable to the world (we put our lamp shade on). Some think the more expensive the clothes, the more they are worth. The more attention we get from the outer appearance, the better we feel about ourselves. We have to get to a point where we are not defined by what is on the outside, because God does not worry about what you are wearing. The only way for His light to shine through you is for it to start shining on the inside. You have to be plugged in just like the lamp. If you are not plugged in to the source, there will be limitations on your life. All of the fine clothes, jewelry, wigs, and weaves will not be able to make your light shine. God is the only source of your strength. We must be plugged into Him in order for our light to shine.

In the same way, let your light shine before men, that they may see your good deeds and praise your Father in heaven. Matthew 5:16

Don't get me wrong, there's nothing wrong with looking good! I like nice things as well. The problem starts when you are defined by what you have on the outside and not by who you are on the inside. This was my problem. I made the mistake of counting my value by what I looked like on the outside. I had a false sense of value. I looked expensive, but was cheap on the inside. Ask yourself this question, are you just living to live or are you plugged into the source and letting your light shine? Waste no more time in your life, we only have one chance to live. Get plugged in and let your light shine!

Chapter 5

Virtuous Woman

Part 1

*B*eing virtuous requires a transformation. It took God's grace and His identity in me to show me my true virtue and to teach me how to walk in it. Virtue is something that all women possess, but some fail to recognize it. I'm not ashamed to say that I haven't always been a virtuous woman. If you want to know what a virtuous woman looks like, let's look at the opposite.

The old me...

I have a spirit of playfulness and joy. You can tell from this photograph that those characteristics didn't always show in my personality or behavior. I also had a dark side. I'm so thankful that God is a forgiving God, because where would I be without Him? I thought I was living my life to the fullest and believed that as long as what I did in the dark never came to the light, that it was okay. In actuality I wasn't living at all. I fooled myself into believing that the lifestyle I lived was exciting and to be envied by others. I played the role of a vixen and not a virtuous woman.

I was a hot mess! It all started with marijuana, alcohol, and boys. I was the quiet and sneaky type of girl. You know, the one that you are supposed to watch out for! Yea, that was me. When I saw something or someone I wanted, I went after it like it was prey. I was a reserved girl by day and a club hopper by night. When I stepped into the room the men all paused; all eyes were on me, and eventually I started receiving VIP treatment. I was living in a fantasy world with realistic repercussions.

I remember a particular night . . . like it was yesterday. I was with my girls when we met some "ques," omega psi phi was my weakness! I met the most desirable man that, at the time, could have been described as *the finest man on earth*. He was so fine that my heart throbbed when I looked at him and I knew that I was going to make him mine... well, at least for that night. We all decided to go to the club together and competition awaited me once I made my entrance with him. Every woman was after this man that

I already locked my eyes on and claimed. I thought I had competition at the club, but to my surprise he locked his eyes on me all night. I was my competitors' envy. He told me that he came with me and that he was going to leave with me. I thought I was so worthy when I heard him speak these words. I thought that I had struck gold! The morning after, we went our separate ways… I never talked to him again and didn't care.

Looking back, I realized that the decisions I made were not wise. I have been left alone. I have even dated several men in hopes to fill a void, but all I got in return was greater emptiness. I felt like a million dollar check that had VOID written all over it. This check had value; you could see the amount; you could hold it in your hand, but it was worthless!

How the precious sons of Zion, once worth their weight in gold, are now considered as pots of clay, the work of a potter's hands.
Lamentations 4:2

God wants you to know that His hands are like erasers. He will erase that void and replace it with His value.

God loves us so much and so unconditionally that one of the ways He showed me my value was through the words of a child. I went to church having great expectations of God. Little did I know I was going to have my own intimate conversation with the Lord throughout the entire service. I was singing, praising, and worshiping God, when this lady turned around and said, "My daughter wants me to give this to you." It looked like a note but it was folded up and on pink paper. I was standing up singing and felt torn to open up this note in the middle of service. I kept singing and said to myself, "I'll just open it when I sit down." It felt like we were standing up for an hour straight. I couldn't resist the feeling to read what was written on the paper. I sat down while everyone was still standing and opened the note. *Here it is, go ahead and read it yourself...*

Dear Virtuous Woman,

I love your outfit and your voice an I really think that you. Should do the tryouts and I would like you to read Zephaniah 3:17 where at says. The LORD your GOD is with you, he is mighty to save, He will take great delight in you, he will quiet you with his love, he will rejoice over you with singing. An you could read Proverbs 31:11-15.

Sincerely,

Taniayah
age:10
4th grade

(P.S. I love your earrings.)

→

You are healed in the name of
JESUS!

Everything that you prayed
for will happen.

After I read the letter from the soul of a child, I was eager to see what was in the scriptures. I didn't know there was a book called Zephaniah, and so I went there first. It reads…

The Lord your God is with you, he is mighty to save. He will take great delight in you, he will quiet you with his love, he will rejoice over you with singing." Zephaniah 3:17

I dug deeper into this scripture and here is what I found…

God was telling me that He was happy with me. It was like when I was younger and received a good report card. The happiness and joy on my parents face was priceless. My report card reflected all the good work that I had done in school, and I knew my parents were proud. Well, this is how I felt when I studied this scripture. The only thing different was that I was shocked to get such a good report. I felt like I didn't deserve it and that I was being given un-merited praise for living in a manner that was unpleasing to God for a long time. Every day, I am my Father's work-in-progress. He is a forgiving God. He will wipe away all of your past sins and throw them into a sea of forgetfulness. Stop being influenced by the devil, because he has no power, remember that! It's not going to be easy but the virtue in you is waiting on you to make a change. If you want God to trust you, you must trust Him first. I have been tested and tried for so long that I had no choice but to make the conscious decision to live as a virtuous woman. This is something that I had to learn. I decided that I was going to really display these qualities in my character. You can do the same. God showed me how to be reverent in behavior, meaning...

My dear brothers, take note of this: Everyone should be quick to listen, slow to speak and slow to become angry. James 1:19

I'm sure you have heard that before, but you can grab onto it and put it into practice if you're not doing so already. God will show you how as you seek Him. I had to learn how to live a chaste life and how to respect myself regardless of how much I desired what was right in front of me. I have become a woman of patience. I learned that your response and reaction to life's unexpected events, demonstrates your character. Part 2 shares why it is so important that we as women live virtuously.

Part 2

I never thought I would be considered a virtuous woman. A year ago, I didn't know what a virtuous woman really was.

Now that I decided to walk in God's light, I have been feeling virtuous. However, I still ask myself the question, "Is this really me?" Here are a few characteristics that I believe describe a virtuous woman: *godly, respectable, chaste, reverent in behavior, and honest.*

This is for the MEN.....

God created you first. Once you become a man, you have obligations in life because God will hold you accountable. You are the head of the household and a wife must submit to you. While, you don't hear this from most pulpits, the Scripture indicates the wife and husband are to submit one to the other. If you will follow God's order and submit to Him, you and your wife should be able to work out any problems you face, assuming you are married to a virtuous woman of God. Part of your obligation is to find that godly wife.

He who finds a wife finds what is good and receives favor from the Lord. Proverbs 18:22

This doesn't mean settling for the first "dime piece" that you see... second, third or fourth. Men, you must ask God to open your eyes so that you can see your rib--your light. When you find your wife, she will have your rib and a light about her that you will recognize. You can't be only focused on her front, back and in between. Focus on what is important. For example, does she have a heart worth more than gold? Will she be a good wife? Will she be a good mother to your children? Will she be a good woman who stands by her husband? You are going to create generations with this woman. This is your bloodline. What are your children's children going to be like? Take time to talk to God before you claim that you found your wife. No one but God will get this right for you. He is the one that created her for you, out of your own rib. God will bring her to you as he brought Eve to Adam in Garden of Eden and Rebecca to Isaac in the Old Testament. It is up to you to find out which woman she is. She is your heart's protector. It's her job; she is your rib! Love her like Christ loves the church. Men, you must also be strong enough to tell your Eve "NO!"-- in a loving way of course. God gives different sets of directions to men than He gives to women. Learn from Adam's mistakes. Be strong enough to redirect your Eve when she has an idea that goes against what God already told you or what you know to be right. This is what women really want: a strong man who listens to God and follows His direction first.

This is for the WOMEN.....

Virtuous woman of God let that light shine! If you are single and desire to be married, you must let your light shine. If your light is turned off, your husband will keep walking right on by you. Ladies, God is the only one who can turn on that switch. Learn how to live and walk virtuously. Don't settle for anything less than what God has for you. The faster you jump in God's arms and stay in Him, the faster He will lead you to your husband. In essence your husband is asleep. Just as Adam was when He brought Eve to him. God will actually lead you to him, but you have to be ready to receive him. Prepare yourself as Esther did. Learn to love God and yourself, so that you will know how to love your husband. There is nothing harder than trying to learn to love yourself, your husband or significant other, and God all at the same time. It just doesn't work that way. You have to take it step by step and God must be first so He can guide you. When you become a wife or if you are a wife, you must understand that you might sometimes have plans and ideas that may not be God's plan for your family. As long as your husband is under God's authority, he will hear orders from God that you will not hear. Trust that your husband wants nothing but the best for you. Submit to him as you submit to God. If submission is difficult for you, pray to God for help. Have faith that God will work out any situation you may find your family in. As a virtuous woman your worth is priceless!

Who can find a virtuous wife?
For her worth is far above rubies. Proverbs 31:10

Learn to love God and you will learn to love yourself. Know that God wants to give you your heart's desires. Why would He give you all that you desire, when you continue to hurt Him? What have you done to God in the past thirty days? Don't say it out loud, because someone might look at you crazy! But despite everything that we have done to Him, He continues to love us. He loves you! You are the apple of His eye. Start pleasing Him, like you are always trying to please Mark, Will, Joe, Ray Ray, and Hakeem! You've been trying to please men that are not even in your life anymore...some of them never were. My single females: A man won't usually leave a friend but will easily leave a lover. So take time to become his friend. Please God and He will never leave you. Even when He isn't pleased, He's still with you and still loves you. Do it for your children, your children's children, and more importantly do it for God.

TAEDRA & BUSHES
(DAIJAH)

TAEDRA & BUSHES

TAEDRA,
MOTHER (SYLVIA)
AND BUSHES

MOTHER,
FATHER (JAMES)
& TAEDRA

SISTER IN-LAW (TRACY)
MOTHER, TAEDRA, FATHER
& BROTHER (CEDRIC)

The Morris Family

Friends

YASHICA & TAEDRA

BRANDY, CODY & TAEDRA

TAEDRA & CHARITY

TAEDRA & TIFFANY

KIM, CHARITY & TAEDRA

CHARITY & KIM

TAEDRA & CODY

Family

RANDALL & LASHELL

UNCLES KENNY, WAYNE, GREG, HAROLD & TONY, CEDRIC & TAEDRA

AUNTIES WENDY & CHRISSY

ALICIA

LASHELL, GRANDPA J, IVY, KENNY, CHRIS,
ALEXIS, JORDAN & BRITTNEE

AUNT PHYLLIS

KIM & STEVIE

UNCLE LEE

Family

LEE & TIFFANY

MONICA

AUNTIE MIGNON, DAD, UNCLE COURTNEY & TAEDRA

Taedra Morris

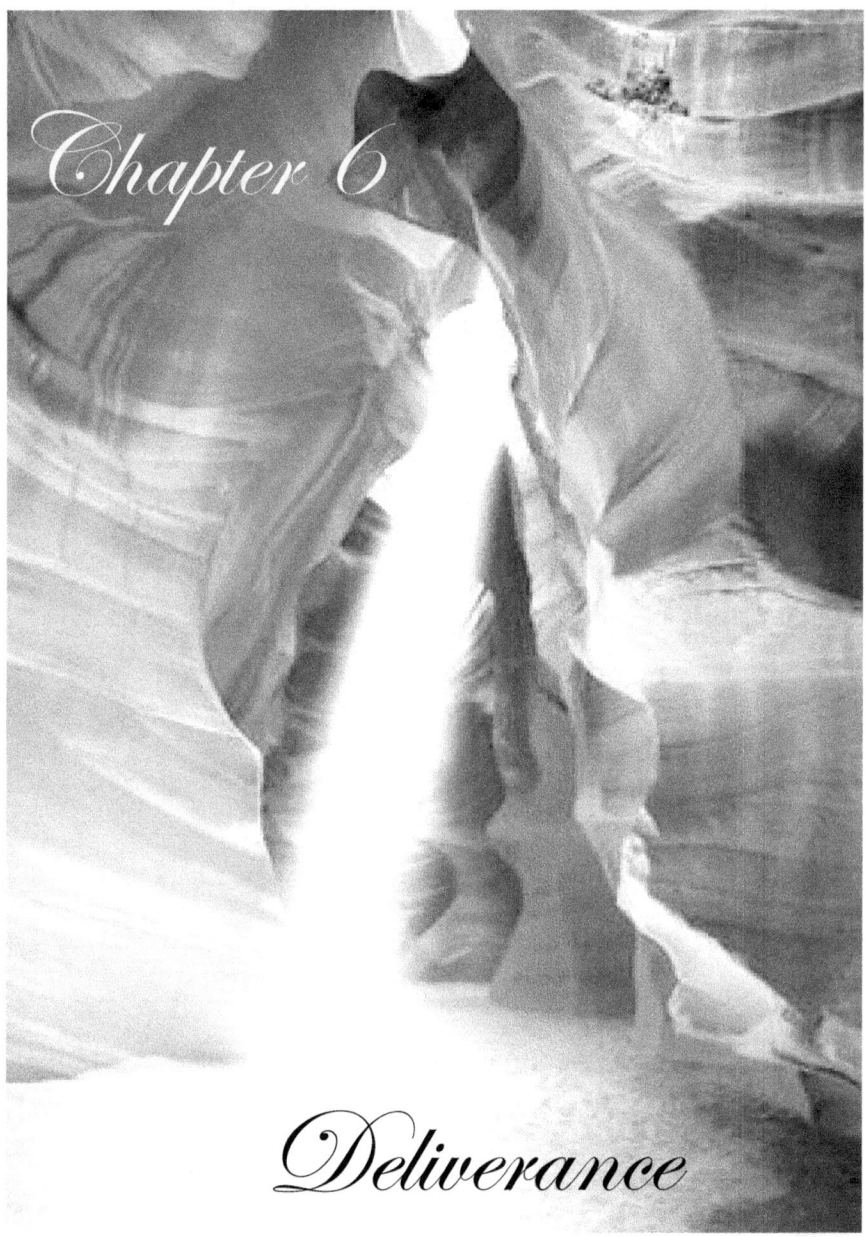

Chapter 6

Deliverance

February 26, 2009, God saved my life and set me free, again at the New Birth singles ministry! I had just walked into the sanctuary and sat down in my seat. I combed the congregation to get a feel of who was present. I saw a woman wearing a black and white checkered jacket and jeans. She had long straight brown hair and her bangs lay straight across her eye brows. For some reason she caught my eye, she looked important, like someone that I should get to know. I remember she had two cell phones attached to her hip, instantly I was drawn to her. Little did I know that God was going to speak to me through this woman, on that very night. Her name is Elder Reona Thomas and there was no doubt left in my mind that she had been sent there by God. She has such a quiet, sweet and caring spirit. I just want to thank her right now for her obedience to our Lord and Savior.

Come with me again to singles ministry...

When Elder Thomas spoke, she asked us all to come to the altar if there was something from which we needed to be set free. I remained in my seat. I tried to convince myself that I was fine. However, no sooner did the thought enter my mind, it also left! I walked down to the altar and said to myself that I was going to receive God. The woman of God spoke in such a calm and quiet voice. She prayed over everyone, and then led us into worship. She lifted her hand in the air and said, "It's time to take three deep breaths! Somebody is going to feel the wind and it's going to be cold. Some of you are going to fall down so make sure you have some room around you."

I thought to myself, "I don't ever fall so I know that she is not talking about me. I'll just position myself to make sure I'm able to catch the person in front of me in case she falls." Again in the quietest voice, almost a whisper, she said, "Take the first deep breath, and then let it out."

I did it! I took a deep breath and then let it out! "That breath was for the breath of the **HOLY SPIRIT**," she said. I was excited because I felt God's presence. I kept worshipping and told myself I'm going to get this!

"Now take the second breath."

I breathed in and out.

"That was the breath of **TRUTH**."

My body became stiff starting at my feet. It was a dry and hard feeling that traveled up my leg, through my knees and up to my torso. It went through my arms and then exited out through my head.

"Take the last breath. This is the breath of **FAITH**."

I stood still at the altar with my arms by my side and my head faced toward heaven. I couldn't move. The next thing I knew I was swaying in the wind. I could still hear my thoughts, while God was shifting my life. I was fighting to stay on my feet but I couldn't control it. I found myself falling gradually backwards to the point that I totally surrendered and landed completely on the floor.

At first I didn't know what was going on. I could still hear everything that was going on around me, but I couldn't open my eyes. The next thing I know I can see two huge, round wide eyes looking at me directly into my eyes. I tried to focus so I could see who it was but it kept quickly moving back and forth so I couldn't get a clear picture. Before I could see anything it disappeared. Right after the eyes disappeared I saw streaks of light. Then once again the eyes were back moving quickly from side to side. This time they were angry! I was scared because I now knew whom the eyes belonged to, and it was mad at me. This time I focused and realized that it was the enemy and he was right in my face, glaring and scowling at me eye to eye. About four different times, it came and went forcefully as if it was trying to ram into a wall so it would fall down. Its colors were black and red; I was so afraid because it just kept growing angrier. I became confused, because I thought I was going to see angels, rainbows, and paradise. But the Lord had an agenda that night! The demon's frown was permanent and it looked as if it had been evicted without notice. It was mad because all of its "stuff" was being put out on the street. It no longer had ownership of my soul and it was pissed off!

The enemy left me that night but kept trying to come back. Every time it made an attempt to get back into what used to be his comfortable home, God blew it away with His own breath. I felt God's breath! It felt cold to my whole body. This is just how much the enemy didn't want to let me go, but God didn't give up on me and blocked satan every time. Satan was trying to kill me! God blew harder and harder every time satan tried to reclaim my soul. I remember the moment that satan let go of me. While I lay there I felt my clothes rippling in the wind. I thought everyone there was cold like me. Has it ever rained on just you? Not usually. So why was I the only one that was cold? All I could feel was the wind and it was so cold I began to shiver. I started to see streaks of light again and it looked as if someone was writing me a message in cursive lettering. I tried to make the words out but I could not see them clearly. The streaks of light soon turned into a flock of birds. I saw them fly up into the atmosphere and when I got a good look at them. I realized that they were doves. I started to hear singing and I felt so much peace come over me. I began to cry because the joy was just so overwhelming. It was a time of rejoicing. I remember laying there and all I could do was cry and smile.

I was set free! Free from all evil dwellings in my body. My greatest release was when I no longer was concerned about a bondage I had carried for years. I no longer felt pain from the loss of my hair. No more doubts of worthiness and no more worrying. It was now time to walk into my promise. God wants me to share my story so that others can be set free. . . just as I was. Is it time for you to walk into your promise?

It is a must that we remember to keep our eyes open when we walk so that the enemies' remnants will not latch on to us while we're just walking down the street; hanging out in ungodly places and such, or tying our souls to ungodly people. Please know that we are bound to walk into some remnants because it's just laid out everywhere we go. Be mindful of what you may have stepped in or touched and know that God will keep you safe as long as you take refuge in Him.

Keep me safe, O God, for in you I take refuge. Psalms 16:1

When God calls you, will you be ready? He calls us every day. Are you hearing Him? Are you ignoring His call? Are you like me? Have you lost something that has you so bound you cannot hear the voice of God? When He says it's time! Will you go? Will you put yourself in an uncomfortable situation to please God? Do you want to continue pleasing yourself or do you want to please God? Most of the time, what God wants you to do is most likely going to put you in an uncomfortable position. Don't be too concerned with what people will say when you say "Yes" to

God and "No" to them. You will have to make some changes in your life. You must learn to be a willing spirit for God that will obey whatever He asks of you. I encourage you to be strong and to hold on to your faith. All things are possible with the Lord.

Your body is the temple of the Holy Spirit and you are a living sacrifice. You are not your own; you've been bought with a price. God wants to save His children and you are a child of God. Are you ready to feel the breath of your heavenly Father? You can run, but you can't hide. God will eventually get your attention one way or another. When He does, let Him use you for His glory.

Chapter 7

I t was the middle of the week and I was worshipping our Lord. After everything that He brought me through, I know that He deserves all the glory and the honor, not only on Sunday, but as often as He blesses and keeps us. This means that you should have continual praise coming out of your mouth for Him. Thanking Him for each breath that you take is not asking too much. God wants you to know that you were born with your "get out of hell free card!" You carry it with you everywhere you go. Yes, you do! You ask what is printed on this card and what does it say?

"The word is near you; it is in your mouth and in your heart," that is, the word of faith we are proclaiming: That if you confess with your mouth, "Jesus is Lord," and believe in your heart that God raised him from the dead, you will be saved. Romans 10:8-9

It's your belief. Do you believe? If you believe, say that verse over again, this time say it and mean it. God knows your sincerity.

For God so loved the world that He gave His only begotten Son, that whoever believes in Him should not perish but have everlasting life. John 3:16

This is what it takes. Salvation is free, but it can only come from God.

For they being ignorant of God's righteousness, and seeking to establish their own righteousness, have not submitted to the righteousness of God. Romans 10:3

You must be sure that the salvation you are seeking is coming from God. This is the first step. You will be tested once you submit and commit to God! If you think your life is always "peachy king" and "fresh like roses," beware, your struggle may be right around the corner. Everything that is worth something is always worth fighting for. As I said earlier, you might have to fight. If things come too easy, be mindful of your situation. It's sometimes harder to do what is right! The enemy doesn't like when you learn the truth. Learn to abide in God's word and you will know the truth.

Then you will know the truth, and the truth will set you free."
To the Jews who had believed him, Jesus said, "If you hold to my
teaching, you are really my disciples. John 8:31-32

The enemy REALLY doesn't like it if you start to walk in faith and believe that God will see you through any situation. You will have some battle wounds because the enemy is not going to give you up easy. This is going to be the fight for your life. Literally!! Satan has fought hard for your life this far and he is convinced that you will never know what you have in God. If he only knew who you really were in the eyes of God, he would leave you alone. God is ready to use you and He wants to make sure that you are a soldier in His army. You can't be weak and defeat the devil. You must learn God's word and know how to use it. We have to put on the whole armor of God in order to defeat the enemy. The bible is your sword. Once you start your journey to strengthen or begin your relationship with God, trust that He will guide you in the direction that you are to go. Let Him lead you into your promise. And leave hell for good....

The fire is still coming down and I lift my head up because that is all the strength that I have left. All of a sudden, I see a glimpse of light. Slowly but surely, I am mesmerized by the light that is shining brightly through the spits of fire, shining brightly in the midst of the rage, and shining brightly in the midst of darkness. As the light grows closer, I look and see that the spits of fire are still there, but the burning sensation is starting to go away. I try to keep focusing on the light, and the more I focus the more the fire doesn't matter anymore. It was still coming down just as heavy and strong as it always did, but I just keep focusing on the light. I stretch my hand toward the light and the wrist that was once drenched in blood is all of a sudden healed and draped in the light. The heat, the enormous heat that I felt upon my body is slowly subdued. I just keep focusing on the light. The more I focused on the light, the more strength I felt enter my body. The light became brighter and brighter and my body jerked up. I placed my hands on the ground and pushed myself up. I took a deep breath and kept focusing on the light. The fire was coming down but it started to fall softer. I just keep focusing on the light. The light met my eyes and traveled through my head. It healed all those areas that were once covered in blood: the blood of despair, the blood of anger, the blood of bitterness, the blood of loneliness, and the blood of depression. The light traveled through my arms and strengthened my broken limbs, then touched my spine and healed all of my infirmities. I felt the calmness with the light and when it reached my legs I was able to stand up. The light healed my body and made me whole. The blood of inequities was being washed away by the blood of Jesus. In the midst of all the fire and what once was pain, I stood up. I keep focusing on the light. I am no longer hot. I am no longer in pain. I am no longer overtaken by the fire. I am no longer dead. It is still raining, but it is no longer burning me. I just keep focusing on the light. I am no longer in bondage! I am free!

The scars remain, but they don't torment me anymore. The light took over my life and I learned that as long as I keep my eyes on the light, it does not matter where I am or what is raining down on me. I later learned why that light was so powerful. Jesus is the light of the world! If you stay focused on Him, you will live life and live it more abundantly. Remember to stay focused on the LIGHT! THE LIGHT OF THE WORLD!

Chapter 8

You Are Victorious

L ife is a race where everyone wins. There are no losers! Whatever situations in which you find yourself, you can win one way or another. You can be victorious in all that you do. It all depends on who is leading your race. What path are you racing on? What choices are you going to make? Run the right race. You will know it is the right one if it is hard! Your race is not going to be easy. You may have been in the same race for forty years. It's not too late! You still have time. God is not in the business of disqualifying. He will give you chance after chance after chance to win. Start repeating this to yourself, "My life is just a race and I have already won!" Speak it into the atmosphere. I was racing against depression. I won that race! I was racing against suicidal thoughts. I won that race! I was racing against low self-esteem. I won that race! I was racing against shame. I won that race! Take a minute and ask yourself what race are you running? How long have you been running this race? It's about time that you conquer it, you are victorious! If you give your race to Jesus, your race will no longer tire you out. There is so much power in the name of Jesus. Think about it, Jesus was running a race, too. Imagine if your race was like

Jesus' race, He endured everything you have and so much more. I'm not sure that anyone would be able to bare the pain that Jesus bore, and to think that He did it all for you and me. Jesus was tempted just like you and I are. The difference is that Jesus did it all without sin. When you are tempted you have to remember this…

When tempted, no one should say, "God is tempting me." For God cannot be tempted by evil, nor does he tempt anyone; but each one is tempted when, by his own evil desire, he is dragged away and enticed.
James 1:13-14

We have to stop straying away from God. Stay focused on Him and He will lead you to victory. The temptation and pain we go through may never equal the pain and suffering that Jesus endured. If He can give His life for us and die, we can give our life to Him and live. Jesus was physically beaten until he was bloody. They stuck a crown of thorns on His head! It doesn't matter how big and bad you think you are, if you get a sliver in your finger, you will stop everything you are doing to get that sliver out! Someone, please get me some tweezers! The same goes for getting something stuck in your teeth. It is imperative that you get it out in order to reduce the pain and irritation that it causes. Let's not mention a paper cut! Isn't it interesting how a thin soft sheet of paper can bring such pain. Stop a minute... and think about what Jesus went through. He went through so much and He didn't even have to! You can press on, too! You can go to God and ask Him to show you how to restore your marriage. You can call on Him in the middle of the night and ask Him to give you peace while you go through withdrawals. You can stop worrying about what your friends and others might think and consider what God thinks. The choice is up to you. God is with you always. The only reason we go through hell, is because we are too stubborn to let go and let God. Stop asking yourself the "why" question. Why me? Why do I have to go through this? Why do I always meet manipulative people? The answer is because you haven't been through enough hell yet in order for you to call out to Jesus. When you have had enough, you will give up and totally surrender to God. If you want to be victorious in all that you do, you must first seek Him. He will give you living water that will quench your thirst forever.

> *Jesus answered, "Everyone who drinks this water will be thirsty again, but whoever drinks the water I give him will never thirst. Indeed, the water I give him will become in him a spring of water welling up to eternal life. John 4:13-14*

You may ask the question, how do I let go and let God? Give God a chance every time you have a feeling of defeat. Ask God to turn that feeling into praise. Give your cares and problems to Him and wait on Him for the answer. Get out your bible and start studying His word. God might not speak to you directly, but there may be someone in your life that has a bit of advice for you, or you might read a sign or billboard you pass, that speaks directly to your situation. God speaks to us in different ways. Surround yourself with godly people and study His word. The Holy Spirit will show you what you need to do once He is convinced that you are serious. I straddled the fence way too long. I had one foot in the church and one foot in the world. I went to church every

Sunday and later started working in the church. I had keys to the church! I could come and go as much as I pleased. Ask me how many times I went to church just to pray and thank Him for what He has done for me. Ask me how many times I went into the sanctuary and got down on my knees just to bask in His glory. Not once! I didn't have a close relationship with God at all. Our relationship was like the friend that had moved far away. Sometimes you think about him/her but never enough to give them a call. This was not my path to victory. Remember, God knows your heart so you can't trick Him. His word says to seek Him first and all things will be added unto you. Once you get into His word He will reveal to you what will come next.

Victory comes through struggle. If there were no struggles, tests, or trials, there would be no victories. Victory is defined as an overcoming of an enemy, the achievement of success in a struggle or endeavor against odds or difficulties. In other words, in order to be victorious you have to go through some tough times. The decisions you make during these hard times will dictate whether you are victorious or not. God gives us free will and it is up to us to choose life.

The thief comes only to steal and kill and destroy; I have come that they may have life, and have it to the full. John 10:10

The key word in this scripture is "may." Other versions of the bible say, "might." This means that life in Christ is not something that is automatic. It's not hereditary or genetic. It is in fact a possibility or probability. You have to put in some work in order to have a life in Christ. It is a choice that you have to make. Think about it like this...

It's kind of like you have to volunteer. Yes volunteer! How much community service have you done? The homeless shelter doesn't come to you and knock on your door. You have to get up and make an effort to go to it. Most of us volunteer because it's something that we want to do. We know that volunteers don't get paid; it's done out of concern and passion. What you get out of it is pleasure; (that is of course, if you were not forced to do it). Living a life in Christ is similar to this. We must learn to volunteer our life to Christ, because it is our passion, not expecting to get paid. Once we submit, we will then receive pleasures from the Lord and have victory in Jesus' name. Once you get to this point, there's no turning back! God will trust you with the victory that He gives you. If you just trust God, He will hide you from your enemies and cover you with His wings. Your life can be full of hope, peace, and victory. I challenge you to trust God with your life today. Receive His refreshing spirit and let the Holy Spirit in you shine through! Remember that "YOU ARE VICTORIOUS!

Chapter 9

I Now Have Joy

There is nothing like the peace and joy that God gives you. Joy unspeakable joy! Joy from depression! Joy from low self-esteem! Joy from the feelings of worthlessness! Joy from addiction!

...as the time when the Jews got relief from their enemies, and as the month when their sorrow was turned into joy and their mourning into a day of celebration...Esther 9:22

God has literally turned my mourning into joy. What the enemy used as leverage to keep me in bondage is now my foot stool for bigger and better opportunities. I can look in the mirror and smile. I can tell my reflection, "You are beautiful, with and without hair." My hair no longer defines who I am. I realize now that I would rather have joy than hair any day! What used to hold me back and keep me captive inside my house inspired me to write this book. God changed my situation so that I would be able to encourage others to embrace what might be holding them back, and to walk in the likeness of God. I had to learn how to embrace my situation; no one but God could get me to do this. There were times when I would be sitting in my house and the doorbell would ring. If I didn't have something to cover up my head, I would run and hide. There was a long, narrow window beside my front door. If anyone was looking inside, they would be able to see me and I couldn't get to my bedroom without walking past the front door. So I just hid and pretended that no one was home. I'm so glad those days are over! I remember walking in the airport for the first time without a wig on. I walked proudly with my head raised high. I literally felt taller. I looked at people in the eye and said, "hello" and gave a friendly smile as I walked past them. I almost started walking like I was on the cat walk. My confidence is restored and I thank God every minute. I had to laugh at myself because this is something that I never thought I would ever be able to do. Actually, I find myself doing many things that I said I would never do. I understand now why people advise you to, never say never. It always catches up to you, and you find yourself doing exactly what you said you would never do.

I encourage you to give God a try. He gave me joy and He will do the same for you. From the moment I let go and let God, I have never been so happy. He will heal every pain and dry every tear from your eyes. He will replace your tears with joy. I shed a lot of tears so I have a lot of joy right now. I never knew that the joy and happiness in God was so overwhelming. Nothing and no one but God could give me this joy, that I never knew existed. My friends and family tried to tell me. I just really wasn't listening, because I was so consumed with the negative. The two people that brought me into this world and love me unconditionally couldn't give me this joy. I thank God for my mother and father (aunt Sylv and uncle James), as everyone calls them. They are my best friends. I thank them for all of their hard work. I know I was a handful to say the least. As much as I love them, my friends couldn't do it. All the men that I confided in, trusted in, and tried to please, couldn't love me enough to bring me this joy that I have. I tried everything to get joy! It took me thirty-one years to finally find it. I even went as far as getting a breast reduction. I believed that this change would solve the problem of low self-esteem, because I would be forced to lose weight. Yes, I felt good after I saw that I had a shape again, but the joy only lasted a moment. I started running out of things to change in order to find joy.

There is no one like the Lord, He is the only one that could give me joy and set me free from all the pain I felt. I will never go back to yesterday; I now look forward to tomorrow. I am excited about my life and what is going to come next! No one can take my joy away! This joy that I have the world didn't give it to me and the world can't take it away.

I remember my first day in the singles ministry. I was torn because I had joined the dance ministry about three weeks prior to my visit. I loved to dance and had danced in my past so I thought this was what I was supposed to do. I spent more than one hundred dollars preparing for this ministry. I fought with myself back and forth. I didn't want to be a quitter, but dance and singles ministry was at the same time on the same day. I had to make a decision. I knew that God had a plan for my life, and after experiencing the awesomeness of singles ministry for the first time, I said to my friend Charity, "I feel like I can't afford not to be here." It has been eight months since joining the singles ministry, and my life has completely changed. I am now on a mission for the Lord and I am so thankful.

May 20, 2009, marked the graduation date of singles ministry. Minister Gray spoke words of shifting on this night. God is a God of timing, and boy was this right on time! It was time to walk in the likeness of the Lord. It was as if we were being prepared to live a life in Christ. We had absorbed all that was necessary in order for us to walk and apply the principles about the goodness of God with His people. God wants us to live a life of joy and peace. Minister Gray said, "It's time for the world to see who you are!" I took these words personally.

Did you know that God's got your back? Literally!

But you will not leave in haste or go in flight; for the Lord will go before you, the God of Israel will be your rear guard.
Isaiah 52:12

Yes, you just read it! I didn't make this up. It's in the bible. God wants you to rejoice in Him, because He has already mapped out your life....all you have to do is follow the map. God is behind you trying to push you in the direction that you are supposed to go. Stop being scared and just move in the direction of His push. It's time to live with joy and an overflow of peace so you can get to a point where it doesn't matter what people say or think. The only thing that should matter is what God says, and what He thinks. He is waiting for you to search for Him. He has always been right there with you. I was tired of crying at night, during the day, at dusk, and then dawn. I was tired of not being able to trust the man who I gave everything I had, and who I thought loved me unconditionally. You know, there came a point where I said enough is enough. It's now finally over! No more headaches and no more heartaches! I am sick and tired of being sick and tired! Aren't you? I can now go to the doctor and not be worried about what my results are going to be. Oh, don't act like you don't know what I'm talking about. I am not the only one that prayed before I got my medical results. There is nothing like the peace and joy that God can give you. I wish I could bottle it up and sell it. I'd make a fortune! Thank you God for saving me! God wants you to go in peace and have joy, unspeakable joy!!

Your turn! Go ahead and reflect on it....

Chapter 1: What Has to Happen

What has happened to you..._____

_____
_____
_____
_____
_____
_____
_____
_____
_____
_____
_____
_____
_____

How does this struggle affect the decisions you make everyday... _____

_____
_____
_____
_____
_____
_____
_____

Are you fed up yet? What are you going to do to let God into your life and start your healing process... _____

_____
_____
_____
_____
_____
_____
_____

Chapter 2: Facade

Name your façade(s.) What do you "put on" to hide from your pain... _____

_____
_____
_____
_____
_____
_____
_____
_____

Write about what you can do to stop hiding... _____

_____
_____
_____
_____
_____
_____
_____

If you do stop hiding how will you feel? Do you trust and believe that God will give you strength and comfort you along the way..._____

_____
_____
_____
_____
_____
_____
_____
_____
_____
_____
_____

Chapter 3: Strongholds

Make a list of your strongholds... _____

_____

_____

_____

_____

_____

_____

Now encourage yourself! Write down how you can overcome each item on that list.
      (Pretend this list is your friends and they are asking for your advice....)

_____

_____

_____

_____

_____

_____

_____

_____

_____

_____

_____

Have you ever settled for less? Write it down and stop settling... _____

_____

_____

_____

_____

_____

_____

_____

Chapter 4:
A Lamp Shade Over Your Light

Get deep with this one. What are your lamp shades, how is this affecting your light..._____

_____

_____

_____

_____

_____

_____

_____

_____

_____

_____

_____

_____

_____

_____

_____

_____

_____

_____

What is your source? Are you plugged in or are you merely decoration... _____

_____

_____

_____

_____

_____

_____

_____

_____

_____

_____

_____

_____

Chapter 5: Virtuous Woman

Explain how you are or can be a virtuous woman or a man of God. What in your life must change... (Oh, come on... this one is serious and it's not easy! Friends, work, words you speak, places you go, food you eat, what you listen to, the way you think...)

_____
_____
_____
_____
_____
_____
_____
_____
_____
_____
_____
_____
_____
_____

Is it worth it to you, to change your life for Christ? Will you be embarrassed to say you changed because you love God? What will you say... _____

_____
_____
_____
_____
_____
_____
_____
_____
_____
_____
_____
_____

Chapter 6: Deliverance

Are you hearing God call you, or are you ignoring His call? When He calls you, will you be ready? _____

_____

_____

_____

_____

_____

_____

What have you lost, that has bound you such that you cannot hear the voice of God...

_____

_____

_____

_____

_____

_____

_____

Are you willing to do what is difficult for you, but pleasing to God? What uncomfortable situation(s) will you have to be in for you to be set free..._____

_____

_____

_____

_____

_____

_____

_____

_____

Chapter 7: Get out of Hell Free

Study to show you're yourself approved! Find out for yourself...Do some research! Do you really know what salvation is? Write down what you think it is..._____

_____
_____
_____
_____
_____
_____

What is the purpose of salvation? Go and look it up! Write down what you find here.

_____
_____
_____
_____
_____
_____
_____
_____
_____

Now when you're ready to surrender and receive salvation from our Father, come back to this page and write about your own experience. _____

_____
_____
_____
_____
_____
_____
_____
_____
_____
_____
_____
_____
_____

Chapter 8: You are Victorious

What race are you running? How long have you been running this race..._____

_____
_____
_____
_____
_____
_____
_____
_____
_____
_____
_____

Are you fully committed or are you still straddling the fence? Ask yourself why and write it down..._____

_____
_____
_____
_____
_____
_____
_____
_____
_____

Have you asked God the "why" question lately? What was your question..._____

_____
_____
_____
_____
_____
_____

Chapter 9: I Now Have Joy

In what situations did God have your back? Has He ever saved your life? Did He heal your body? Has He ever kept your family safe? Did He provide food for you to eat when you were hungry? Has he ever kept you out of harms way? I'm sure God has done so much for you, do some reflecting and write it down..._____

_____

_____

_____

_____

_____

_____

_____

_____

_____

_____

_____

_____

_____

_____

_____

_____

_____

_____

_____

_____

_____

_____

_____

_____

_____

_____

_____

_____

_____

Now, write your prayer to God and thank Him for having your back...

_____
_____
_____
_____
_____
_____
_____
_____
_____
_____
_____
_____
_____
_____
_____
_____
_____
_____
_____
_____
_____
_____
_____
_____
_____
_____
_____
_____
_____
_____Amen.

Appendix 1:

This book contains scripture quotations from the Holy Bible.

All translations come from the New International Version.

Chapter 1
What Has To Happen
1. 1John 4:16

Chapter 2
Facade
1. Matthew 6:34
2. Ezekiel 37:1

Chapter 3
Strongholds
1. Revelations 21:6
2. Romans 12:2
3. Matthew 6:33
4. Joshua 6:3-20
5. 2 Timothy 3:12
6. Isaiah 45:1

Chapter 4
A Lamp Shade Over Your Light
1. Matthew 5:16

Chapter 5
Virtuous Woman
1. Lamentations 4:2
2. Zephaniah 3:17
3. Isaiah 38:17
4. James 1:19
5. Proverbs 18:22
6. Proverbs 31:10

Chapter 6
Deliverance
1. Psalms 16:1

Chapter 7
Get out of Hell Free
1. Romans 10:8-9
2. John 3:16
3. Romans 10:3
4. John 8:31-32

Chapter 8
You are Victorious
1. James 1:13-14
2. John 4:13-14
3. John 10:10

Chapter 9
I Now Have Joy
1. Esther 9:22
2. Isaiah 52:12

**** Don't forget ****

I would love to hear your thoughts.

Share your comments with me at:
www.hellisnotalwayshot.com

www.ingramcontent.com/pod-product-compliance
Lightning Source LLC
LaVergne TN
LVHW021402080426
835508LV00020B/2407